AF316836

The Awesome Companion Book for

JUNIOR JUGGLERS

Games to prepare young jugglers

By Mike and Gail Murphy

Contents

WHAT IS AN AWESOME COMPANION BOOK?

The Awesome Companion Books are a series "How To" guides for children and adults. Each book in the series

has a companion book designed for children. However, the books can be used independently.

As the adult learns they assist the child on their similar journey through the same topic. Each book has cross over activities where both adults and children work through activities in the book together.

Everyone has fun in an engaging learning activity that also serves to strengthen the bond and connection between both learners.

When you see this symbol this is an opportunity to share an activity or game with your companion. Both The Awesome Companion Book for Junior Jugglers and The Awesome Companion Book for Jugglers feature numerous companion projects with the idea that both of you will work together and help each other learn.

EARNING LEVELS

As you complete activities in this book you earn achievement levels.

LEVEL ONE

Blue Elk

LEVEL TWO

Red Fox

LEVEL THREE

Gator

LEVEL FOUR

Silver Hawk

LEVEL FIVE

Gold Dragon

I Want to be a Juggler

Ever see a juggler at a carnival or on a street corner or a show and think "That's pretty awesome, I'd like to do that". Well guess what, you can!
Juggling is great fun but it does take practice. Each activity in this book is designed to help you learn how to throw and catch a ball with one hand, both hands, and with a partner. You will develop better hand/eye coordination (meaning your hand and eye will work together quicker). So practice, play and most of all have fun.

Practice Balls

We recommend using a "stress ball" for most of the activities in this book. You can roll, toss and bounce stress balls. Plus, you can bounce them off a wall without leaving a mark. (believe me, I found out the hard way). If you use tennis balls or bouncy balls you will spend a lot of time chasing them around the house.

Later in this book, you will want to use a ball that can bounce, but not too high. (even though high bouncing balls are pretty awesome). You can find them at department or dollar stores.

EXERCISE ONE
Roll one ball between hands

Stretch your legs out against a wall and roll the ball between your hands. Keep your hands about two feet apart with your palms facing each other. Let the ball roll easily into your hands and try not to bat the ball.

Practice this several times until you can do it with your eyes closed.

EXERCISE TWO
Bounce ball between hands

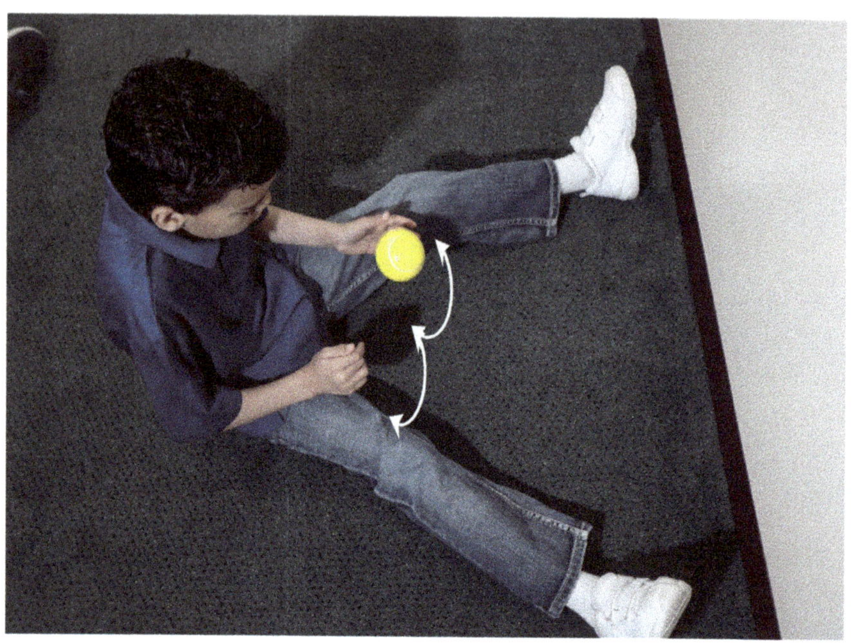

You're already sitting on the floor so let's try something different. Instead of rolling the ball between your hands, bounce the ball back and forth.

You have to find the right bounce. Not too high so you can't catch it and not too low so it hardly bounces at all. Try to bounce the ball as high as your eyes and try and keep your hands by your sides to catch the ball.

Can you do it with your eyes closed?

     The Awesome Companion Book for Junior Jugglers

You have achieved level one
You are now a **Blue Elk.**

EXERCISE THREE
Rolling the Ball Against the Wall

With your legs in a sitting position against a wall roll the ball so it hits the wall and rolls back to you. Try not to roll the ball so hard that it bounces (bouncing is in exercise four) but keep a steady, consistent roll.

Try rolling with just your right hand several times and then switch to your left hand. Next, roll from one hand to the other. Keep practicing until you can consistently control the ball.

     The Awesome Companion Book for Junior Jugglers

EXERCISE FOUR
Bounce one ball off the wall

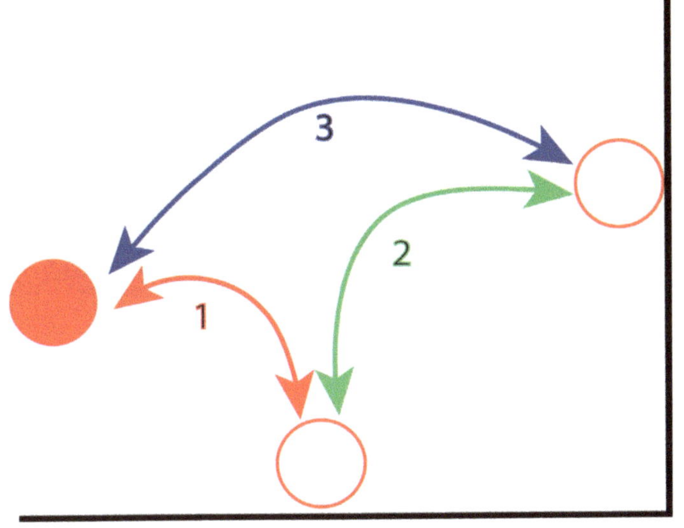

Now for something just a little bit harder. With your legs in a sitting position against a wall toss the ball so it bounces off the floor, off the wall, and back to you.

With practice the ball qill bounce back to you so you can easily catch it. Practice how hard you throw the ball, where the ball hits the floor and where the ball hits the wall. Once you can bounce the ball consistently, try switching to your other hand.

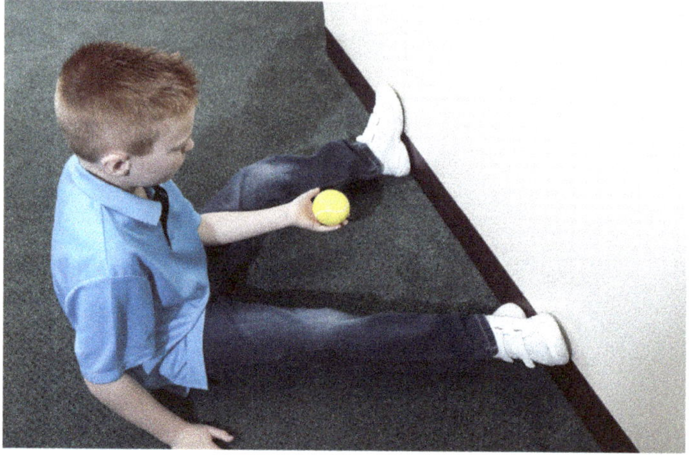

Don't throw so hard that the ball flies over your head

Bounce the ball off the wall so it comes right back to your hand.

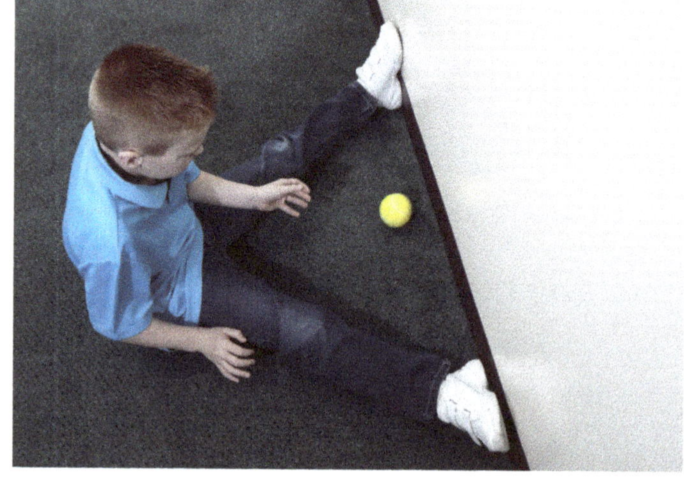

Go back and forth between your right hand and your left hand.

Here is a great opportunity for your companion to sit with you and play the same games.

You can help each other with suggestions and share tips on how to improve.

Your companion can also counts the number of times you toss and catch the ball and note each time you do better.

EXERCISE FIVE
Bounce Two Balls off the wall

For twice the fun, try bouncing two balls off the wall. Start with one hand and once the first ball bounces back then toss the second ball with the other hand.

Try and keep a rhythm going. Bounce to the beat of your favorite song.

Can you alternate hands, throwing with one hand and catching with the other?

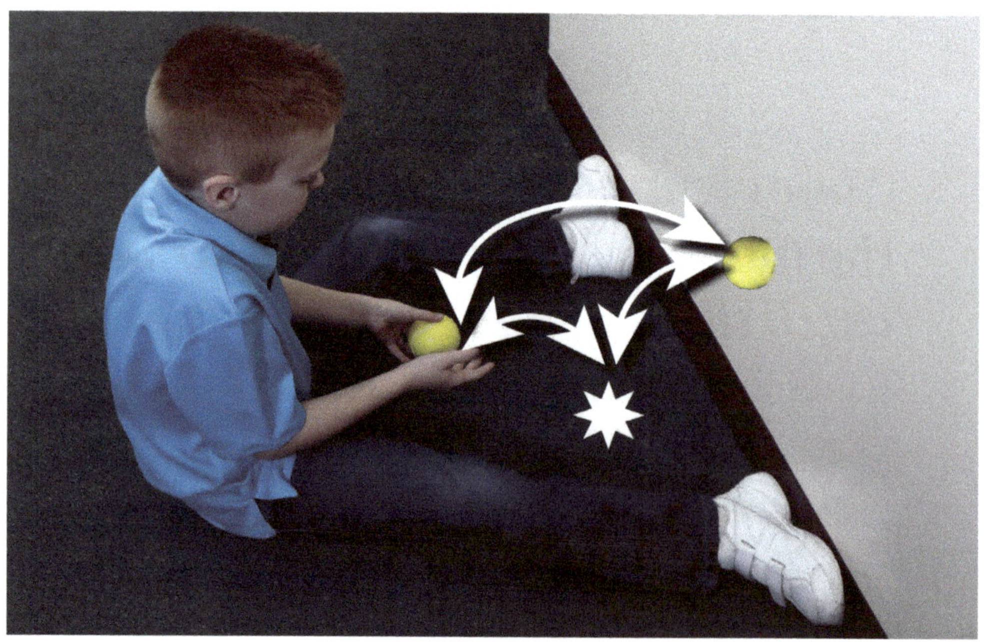

CONGRATULATIONS!

You have achieved level two
You are now a **Red Fox**

EXERCISE SIX
Standing Ball Toss

 Now it's time to stand up straight. Toss the ball straight up to eye level with and catch it with the same hand.

Try to look straight ahead as you toss and catch and let the ball fall into your cupped hand. Don't clutch the ball tightly. In juggling, the balls continually drop and leave your hands so it is important that you can toss the balls quickly and easily.

How many times can you toss the ball without dropping it?

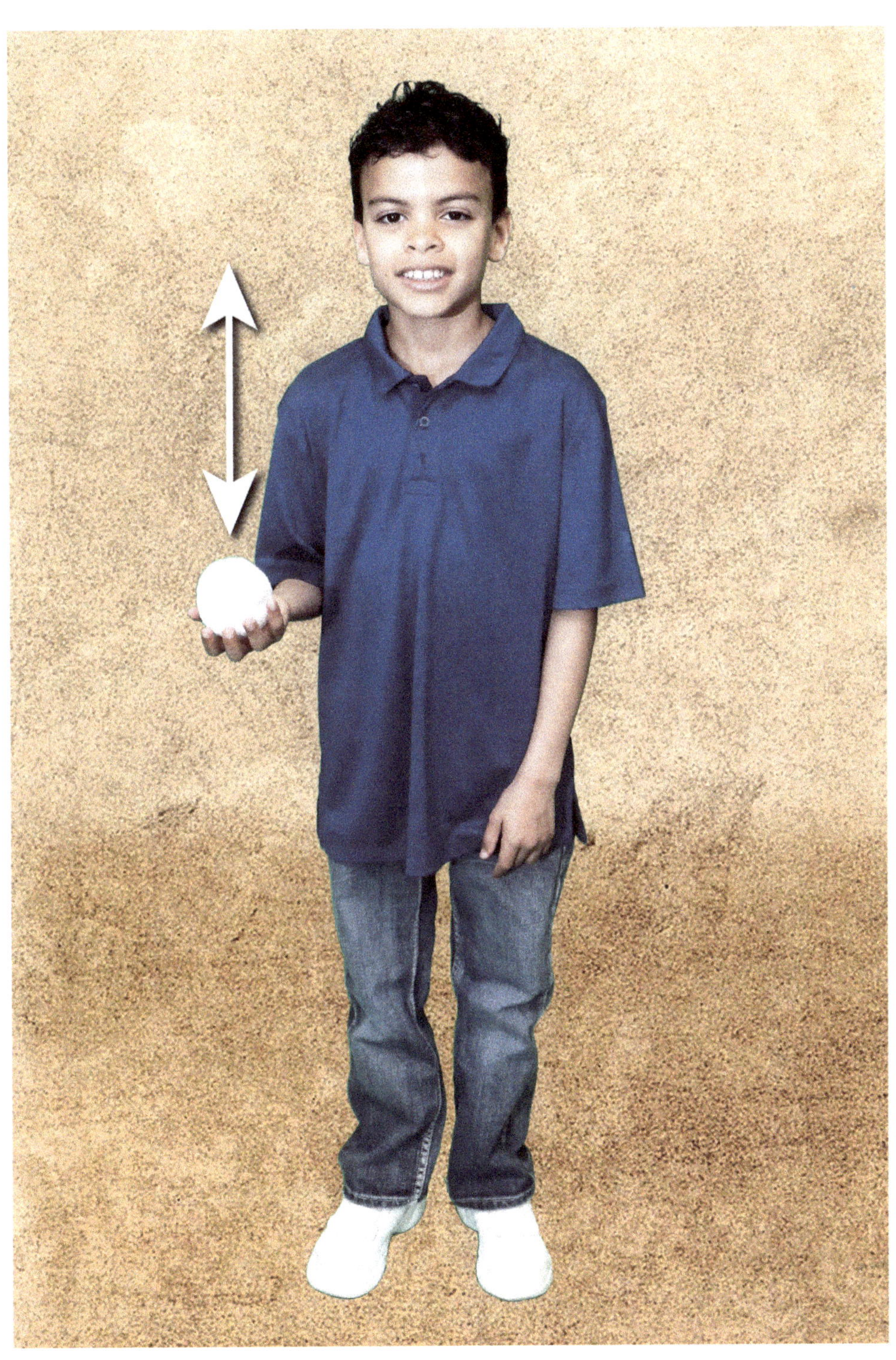

We recommend practicing each exercise until you can do it without thinking. In many activities we suggest closing your eyes while rolling or tossing the ball.

Get your companion to help you. Once you feel you have mastered an activity, have your companion watch you as you attempt to perform the same activity with your eyes closed.

Of course jugglers don't perform with their eyes closed will help you develop your muscle memory.

see page 33 in the Awesome Companion Book of Juggling

EXERCISE SEVEN
Ball Bounce Underhand

Now is the time to find that bouncy ball. The one that doesn't bounce too high or too low. Keep both hands, palm up and hold the ball in one hand. Drop the ball hard enough so the ball bounces up so you can easily catch it in your hand.

First bounce and catch with one hand then switch to the other hand. Then bounce from one hand to the other.

"This is the last time we use the mega super bounce ball".

Hold the ball palm up. This is the standard hand position for juggling.

Bounce the ball high enough to reach your hands.

Practice with one hand then later practice with the other hand.

Check This Out

When you are standing and bouncing the ball make sure you are standing straight. Don't reach down or bend down to catch the ball.
If you find you are always bending to catch the ball, find a ball with a better bounce.

CONGRATULATIONS!

You have achieved level three
You are now a **Green Gator**

    The Awesome Companion Book for Junior Jugglers

**On page 22 of the
Awesome Companion Book of Juggling
we recommended some light warm up
and muscle building exercises.**

**You will find out that all the activities
in this book stretches and strengthens
your arms.**

**Work with your companion and develop
a warm up program to get your muscles
ready to juggle**

TWO

 The Awesome Companion Book for Junior Jugglers

PERSON

EXERCISE EIGHT
ROLL BALL - ONE HAND

Practicing with one ball by yourself is a lot of fun, but it's even more fun if you can play with another person. Find a friend, sibling, parent or a very smart pet (kidding) to help you with these activities.

For exercise eight, sit on the floor facing each other. Roll a ball straight to the other person's hand. If you are rolling from your right hand the other person would catch the ball in their left hand. Keep practicing right to left, left to right.

Now, try rolling the ball to opposite hands, right to right, left to left. Keep a consistent rhythm going. LIghtly catch the ball each time. Try not to bat the ball back.

Next, try something more challenging by moving farther apart from each other.

Roll the ball straight. Practice with one hand then switch to the other.

Roll the ball to opposite hands. Switch hands back and forth.

Try to keep the same pace with each roll. When you feel ready, roll the ball faster.

EXERCISE NINE
Ball Bounce - One Hand

Place a large ring in-between you and your partner. This can be a toss ring, a cut out paper plate or whatever will work as a target on the floor. Your partner then bounces the ball into the ring and back to you. Bounce the ball into the ring and up to your partner.

Bounce the ball from your right hand to your partner's left hand then switch hands. The goal is to find the right amount of bounce so both of you can easily catch it without having to reach high or low. Toss the ball underhand and catch it as you did in exercise six.

As a challenge, try moving farther away from each other while keeping control of the ball.

Can you alternate hands?

CONGRATULATIONS

You have achieved level four
You are now a **Silver Hawk**

Check This Out

When you practice each activity in this book, keep track on how many times you can roll, toss or bounce the ball without losing control. Ten times today, maybe fifteen times tomorrow!

EXERCISE TEN
Ball Bounce Two Balls

Let's get a little crazier. This time bounce two balls at a time,
one after the other. Each person holds a

bouncy (but not too bouncy) ball. You start by bouncing your ball in the middle circle. When that ball hits the circle the other person bounces their ball to you. Create a good rhythm. If it is hard to toss and catch try moving farther apart.

How far can you go and still hit the center of the ring?

Next, you and your partner try tossing the ball into the ring at the same time.

Are you quick enough to both toss and grab the ball?

An important part of learning to juggle is arching the ball between your hands.

Have your companion work with you on mastering the arch toss. You need to learn this before moving on to juggling.

See page 23 in the Awesome Companion Book of Juggling

EXERCISE ELEVEN
One Ball Toss - Standing

What are you sitting down for? It's time to stand up and stretch your legs. This is a simple game of catch but with a difference.

Instead of tossing the ball straight ahead, toss the ball in a criss cross pattern to the other person who then tosses it back to you.

Get a good arch on the ball when you toss it to the other person. When you can repeatedly toss the ball back and forth without dropping

then switch to the other hand.

I know we mentioned this many times but it is important. Keep your palms facing up and keep the ball loose in your hands. You will be able to toss the ball quicker and easier which will be very important once you graduate to three ball juggling

EXERCISE TWELVE
Two Ball Toss - Standing

Take two balls, one for each person. First you toss the ball to your partner then your partner tosses the other ball to you. Practice going faster and moving further away while still keeping control of the ball.

Next, try tossing the balls to each other at the same time. This will really challenge your hand/eye coordination. Keep count on how many times you can toss and catch without dropping the ball.

"Hey, I don't throw the ball that hard".

Make sure you keep a nice arch.

Both ball should have the same arch height.

How many times can you toss without dropping one or both balls?

CONGRATULATIONS

You have achieved level four
You are now a **Gold Dragon**
and you are ready to learn to
juggle!

EXERCISE ONE
One Ball Arch

Now that you've learned how to roll, bounce and catch one and two balls, it's time to move on to beginning juggling.

In the Awesome Companion Book of Juggling (page 23) the first exercise is the One Ball Arch. Learning the One Ball Arch is the first step on the road to three ball juggling.

Keep the hands straight out from either side of your body and try not to move your hand closer together or move the arm up to catch the ball. Try and toss the ball between your hands, in an arch, as high as your eyes.

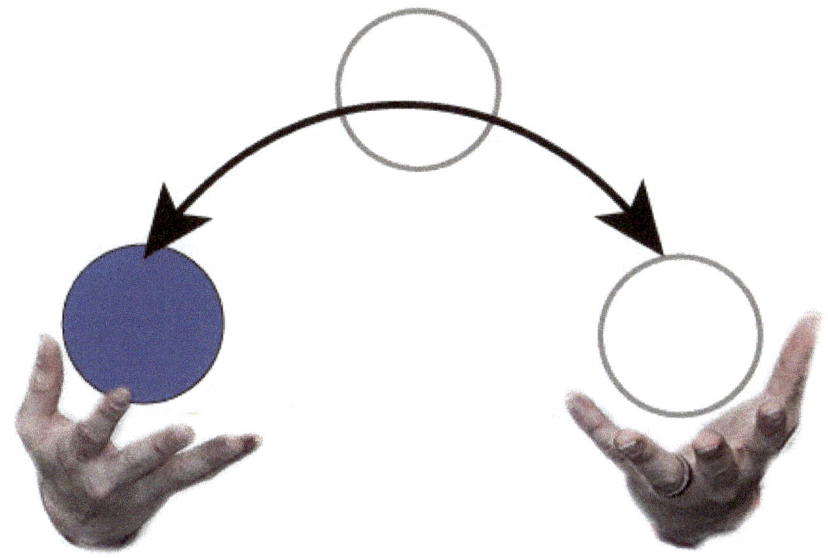

This picture above shows how to toss the ball from the right hand to the left hand. Try and keep your hands open and don't grab the balls when you are catching them.

Try counting one....two....one.... two to help you get a good rhythm going. Count how many times you can catch the ball without dropping and try and do better with each toss.

A great way to share ideas and have fun working together is to make something. For this project you should work with an adult or older friend and make your own juggling balls.

You can decorate them anyway you want and they are excellent for tossing, catching and beginning juggling.

You will need to use scissors so it is important that you work with and adult.

MAKING BALLS

Here's how you can make your own juggling balls. Although these homemade balls aren't very good for bouncing and rolling, they're great for catching and juggling

Tools Needed
Scissors
Fold and close sandwich bag
At least six 12 inch balloons
A funnel
Rice, birdseed or sand
Assorted stickers

First get 2 twelve inch balloons preferably of different colors

Cut the tip of both balloons.

Fill a fold and close sandwich bags with one of the following fillers: birdseed, rice or sand. Rice is a preferred filler. If you use birdseed make sure there are no large seeds that could tear the ball from the inside. Sand works but your juggling balls will be much heavier. Fill the bag about ¾ full.

Take the tip of the balloon and use it to close the bag. Insert the bag into one of the balloons and pull the balloon over the filled sandwich bag.

Take the other balloon and pull it over the first juggling ball. Take the tip you cut off and use it to close the sandwich bag of material

Insert the bag into one of the balloons and pull the balloon over the filled sandwich bag. Take the other balloon and pull it over the first juggling ball.

Decorate the balls with stickers. You can also cut small holes in the outer balloon revealing the inner balloon colors.

You have made your own juggling ball. Just repeat the process two more times.

But if you're impatient or don't have any balloons you can always use rolled up socks in the meantime time.

**That's what I get for filling
my juggling balls with birdseed**

ABOUT THE AUTHORS

Andy Murphy is an accomplished juggler and musician. He has been juggling for more than 14 years and is a proud member of the International Juggling Association. Andy is the co-founder of the BCR juggling club in Kenosha, Wisconsin. Andy resides in Kenosha, Wisconsin with his wife, Emilie and daughter,

Mike Murphy is also a 14 year veteran of juggling and co-founder of the BCR juggling club. Mike lives in Kenosha, Wisconsin with his wife, Gail.

Oh, and he's Andy's father.